Bard Unmasked

Lisa Goodwin

Wizards of Avalon

2022

Acknowledgements

The Elder Bards and Gorsedh of Ynys Witrin,
The Fellowship of The White Spring.

This book is dedicated to all who care for the
sacred places, my former self and others reflected
in these words, including you.

With thanks to my family,
Mum, Max, Lauren, Jack, Beth and Kai,
and practically everyone I know in Glastonbury,
along with some I don't know,
who continue to inspire me.

Contents

Bard

Remnants of a Girl

Shades of Woman

Echoes of Family

Rebel Teacher

Shapes of a Poet

Reluctant Priestess

The Druid's Prayer

Grant, Oh Spirit,

Thy Protection;

And in protection, strength;

And in strength, understanding;

And in understanding, knowledge;

And in knowledge, the knowledge of justice;

And in the knowledge of justice, the love of it;

And in that love, the love of all existences;

And in the love of all existences,

the love of God, Goddess and all goodness.

Introduction

Lisa Goodwin is the 8th Chaired Bard of Gorsedh Ynys Witrin and winner of the Glastonbury Festival Poetry Slam 2019. She recently founded Avalon Wizard Academy, her online realm of magic, and she supports The White Spring Fellowship and their aims to maintain sacred sanctuary at the base of Glastonbury Tor.

Initiated as a Bard of Caer Avebury in 1999, but it was not until 13 years later that she took to the stage with The Legend of Prometheus, and won the Ynys Witrin Bardic Chair. Since then she has written and performed a great many poems.

Lisa's mission is to elevate the word, and more than that, to show that a magical way of life is not only possible, it is essential.

She wants you to know that both magic and poetry can be raw and spontaneous and doesn't have to take forever, or be complicated. Part of her mission is to encourage other folk to explore and express their own creative power and allow The Awen to flow.

"The Awen is the central symbol of Druidism. It is formed by three rays of light and sound, which represent the three drops of wisdom that flew out of Ceridwen's cauldron and provided Taliesin with divine inspiration.

It represents the triplicity of all things, essentially, Love, Truth and Justice. It is used to invoke divine inspiration from the Muse. Awen is a Welsh word derived from the Indo-European root 'uel' meaning 'to blow'. It has the same root as 'Awel' the Welsh word for breath. There is a related word in Irish 'ai' which also means 'poetic inspiration'."

www.ynyswitrin.org.uk/wisdom/

Foreword

Thank you for buying my book. It has been a long time in the making and now I am ready to let it out into the world. You will find the favourites here, Taliesin, The Legend of Prometheus, and I want to move to Glastonbury.

These classic performance pieces stand alongside more intimate poems of a girl growing up in NW London, daughter, mother, lover, rebellious teacher and reluctant priestess.

I was given a compliment this summer when a young man told me, "When you are dead, your poems will be of much worth."

This, of course, will only be true if I get them out of their dusty notebooks and out of the mess of computer files to put them in books. So this first book is for you kids, there are more to follow. I hope he is right!

"Publishing a book of poetry is like dropping a rose petal down the Grand Canyon and waiting for the echo"
— Don Marquis.

It may float and drift on the wind, softly catching the updrafts to swirl in the air. Even if no-one looks up to see it, the rose petal expresses itself with beauty and grace.
May you find some of the same here.

Bright blessings, Lisa Goodwin.

BARD

Hail the Bard, They Say.

And I would while the day away,
If you would bid me, stay.
I would taste the bitter sweet,
The warmth of love, the cold retreat.

Yes, I would tarry on the stage,
And tear the words out from the page.
To bring them forth with foolish tongue,
Yes, I would still both moon and sun.

For what cold stare can halt the flowing,
Of bardic stoic poets knowing?
And what fairy feet can trip the beat?
What seeds of truth are worth sowing?

What words are left worth saying?
What prayers unsaid still need praying?
While stories unfold and old tales are told,
What bardic fool is worth the paying?

And what words may I say to you,
To let you know my heart be true?
Deep felt thoughts and fancy stanzas,
Or lustful tales once thought taboo?

What may leave you open mouthed,
Like hungry new born babe?
What sultry language can arouse,
A burning effervescent flame?

What will unlock your bleeding heart,
And leave you overawed?
What will blow your mind apart,
And move you to applaud?
And while I while the day away,
Will you hark my voice?

When I find something to say,
Will it still internal noise?

For truly, it's not study or knowing,
That births these words to form.
Simple surrender to the flowing,
Of Awen dancing with a bard newly born.

So hark, here's my confession,
I have a year to lift the word,
But this brand new profession,
In truth, is profoundly absurd!

I have no study to lean upon,
No instrument for melody to sing a song.
No thing to hang myself upon,
Just me, myself and foolish tongue.
And I'm making it up as I go along.

The Legend of Prometheus

Always reaching for the light that bold Prometheus,
Refused Titanic fight, spared the jail in Tartarus.
He spent night after night with his brother Epimetheus,
Shaping man after might in name of his love.

And so by his design and his love for all humanity,
He shaped mankind then, no mere technicality,
Athena was consigned to breathe life; mortality.
Human being was defined but what of personality?

Endurance, strength and nerve, an afterthought to give
To the creatures of the earth, Epimetheus's gift,
but it never does occur to give humankind a lift,
and Prometheus observes this rift.

Epimetheus's cup had nothing left for man.
The animals all supped, from the lion to the lamb,
but we were snubbed in favour of his plan.
So Prometheus stood us up and the resistance began!

He felt his love for humans like fire in his brain
and under no delusion he nurtured tender flame.
To bring it to his people to rise against their pain
and a way to keep all of us warm in wind and rain.

Zeus declared that sacrifice must be more robust.
He took the best of the flesh and left the rest for us,
So Prometheus did a trick and the jape was later sussed,
and with only bones to pick, Zeus took fire, left us dust.

Prometheus flew higher than Icarus, and even though it stung,
with treachery vociferous, he lit a torch from the sun.
Imagine the aurora! Yes! Zeus was set to stun.

He sent pretty Pandora, deceptive heart and lying tongue.
And a funny looking box that should never be undone
Oh, what a stunning beauty was sent to live among
Athena, Epimetheus, Prometheus and us.

Pandora's curiosity was bound to do us in.
Her apparent generosity was not to be boxed in.
And she unleashed an atrocity of suffering and sin.
and all manner of monstrosity to get under our skin.

Now it is debatable, who left us with false hope
so we could be capable to cope.
Was it he in chains unbreakable or that dope
of a woman, unobtainable, who revealed the box's scope.

Yes. He in chains unbreakable. Immortal mortal male.
Prometheus' unmistakable apparent epic fail
Made his freedom unsustainable, his passion was curtailed.
He was seized by Gods unshakable, chained on Caucasian jail.

Day and night tormented by a giant eagle's need,
Prometheus never repented. 'Liver heal and liver bleed!'
Man, I would go demented while the hungry beast did feed,
Yet Prometheus never lamented it's greed.

Then Zeus gave two conditions for his freedom to be met.
If he could proposition and somehow get
an immortal volunteer to agree to be dead,
and a mortal so sincere to destroy the daily threat.

Then in walked tender Chiron and brave Heracles.
The trickster may find asylum with God's such as these!

With a sweet surrender and sudden irony,
wounded healer and defender died with notoriety.
It was no small labour, but the mortal killed the bird
And unchained poor Prometheus ... at least that's what I heard.

Until today, when I met him on the bus!
Yes, I know it's an unlikely place for people like us.
Still I took the chance to ask him, 'why Prometheus?'
And he told me ...

"I Prometheus, wild adversary,
Thief Immortal, paradoxical trickery.
I bring you Fire! I offer Power!
Bring you liberation to create or to devour.

I, Titanic traitor chained unto a stone.
Bird satiator, cursed to live and die alone.
Yes, my fate was always marred, the gate to Olympus barred,
permanently scarred, and on what charge?

My unrepentant, holy, burning heart.
He despised my cunning, he shunned my art,
Why? Because I dared!

Bound in chains, my Olympic fall from grace.
Each day, an eagle's feast, my sacrifice to warm your face.
Why? because I cared!

And a thousand vestal virgins, do not do me honour,
and a million clay built humans still shun the sacred fire.
Why?

Well don't just stare!
You heard me! I gave up what I got!
I suffered and I sacrificed, for what?!

You! Yes, you! Clay built flora in God's image,
tormented by Pandora, holding false hope's privilege.
I conspired, I inspired you to take charge of your own.
To stand against authority, to take wisdom gods have known.

And now little metal boxes warm your heart and heat your homes,
Orange coiling filaments, light switches. Flame dis-owned!
And you choke in the smoke of your ill fed bonfires.
Eyes burning acrid; blinded by fools and liars.

And like Zeus, you bind me! Another rock to sit upon.
You stand me in eternal golden form,
beside your temple to Mammon.
Rockerfella wraps me in a zodiacal chain,
To witness your torture again and again.

All you vacant vestal virgins wear about your neck, false chains.
And my deluded clay creations. You know nothing of my pains.
Do you? Or do I judge too quick?

Will you awaken from the eternal torture of your soul?
Will you break the chains that bind you before your liver is sold?
Will you tend a sacred flame? Will you keep it pure and clear?
Take the power of my prophecy to those who would hear!

Will you light a simple fire, to sit by with your friends?
Will you grasp your sovereignty? You have a planet to mend.
Do you dare to burn and sack your Gods of corporation?
Do you care to claim back? Reinstate your sovereign nation!

I Prometheus,
A living mythology.
In the darkness of mystery,
I leave with you, my history.
Complete it!

The Bard Appears to Be

The Bard knows when to speak, when to be quiet.
Never appearing to be silent,
Or disappearing in the face of a riot.

A deer in the mist won't appear at your will,
Nor will it at all if you can't be still,
At one with nature, peaceful, fulfilled.

No conflict in the coming or the going.
No disparity twixt knower and the knowing,
With faith in the Truth in the shadow on a stone.

Discipline and wisdom to keep your mouth shut.
Not ducking at the sign of the first gun shot,
Only coming back, resurrected, love.

The Bard appears to be hidden in the deepest mist,
The Bard appears to be riding on the narrative,
The Bard appears to be standing on a precipice.

Repairing tattered wings and preparing them to fly.

The Truth

I'd like to introduce you to the truth.
But she came naked,
Screaming from the well.
Her rage fulfilled by falsity,
Looking like she'd come from hell,
To raise a wild cacophany.

Well, she had so much to say
And she wouldn't be contained
By shyness, shock or shame.
I let her in, but she clawed at my skin.
Told me strength can lie in suffering.
Power can lie in understanding.

In truth, all lies will shatter silence.
But a tree not rooted in honesty,
will fall in foul weather.
I offered food and clothing.
Fragments of philosophy,
Ribbons of story.

We talked of Plato,
Aristotle and Socrates.
We pinned together
patches of parable
With threads of allegory,
Dressed up in metaphor.

We considered the complexity
Of bare naked truth.
Then she gave me poetry,
And handed me the broom.

Taliesin

Nature applauds us with cheers of thunder,
And cascades of rain. Every moment under,
Her grasp, so tenacious, she threatens to take me.
To devour and love me, yet forsake me.
Gwion am I who took from her cauldron,
The three blessed drops of pure inspiration.

Oh, she is not happy, she's making a fuss.
She will tear me apart, I know that I must,
Flee the Enchantress, so crooked, yet fair.
There beats in my chest, the heart of a hare.
I dart over the earth with a bitch on my heel.
The start of a quest to discover what's real.
And so I embark on my fateful folly;
Seeking to find I am not my body!

Rain claps the river and cold water beckons,
My sense of self just another obsession,
I dive in the water, my heart skips a beat,
As my salmon body leaps into the deep.
Transformed into otter, she threatens to eat me,
Still, I am determined she won't defeat me,
So I sweep through the rivers and scale the oceans;
Seeking to find I am not my emotions!

Now cold blue lightning lashes the water,
And I know that the otter bitch will not falter.
So fins turn to wings and I take to the air,
Hearing the birds sing of freedom up there,
Her hawk eye is on me. She's still on my back,
Clipping my feathers and poised to attack!
I look to the wind, ask how I'm defined.
Only seeking to find I am not my mind!

And now as my body descends from the flight,
The clouds reveal a crescendo of light,
And riding it's rays, I blaze into the corn,
I await the goddess, I will be reborn.
Surrendered, devoured, I am not beaten,
As by the holy Ceridwen I am eaten.
I look to my mother to ask what I got,
Only seeking to find, I am not, I am not, I am not!

I grow in her belly, a year and a day,
I am birthed and re-birthed, and then cast away.
Swaddled in crane skin, thrown in the sea,
There I come to All knowing, or it comes to me.
And there stops my seeking and wishing to be,
For what I am seeking is resting in me.
And as you can tell by the fire in my head,
I am the Bard Taliesin; Thrice blessed.

Scheherazade's Lamp.

The lamp is lit and there's a tale to tell tonight,
So come and take a seat beneath my spell tonight,
By Bab Mansour, I found this magic lamp,
My heart's desire yearning to be quelled tonight,

God and I, through coloured glass, bear witness,
While whispers fill this wall-girt citadel, tonight.
He speaks the things that never must come out,
Says, tell the tales, and raise a merry hell, tonight.

While I remain enthralled by smokeless fire,
He speaks of Madames and their jezabels tonight.
As darkness is illuminated by her deeds,
Bones tumble 'neath the fig tree by the well, tonight.

The mysterious host of ghosts, alive in flesh,
Will know who's buried in the hot sand hills tonight.
No hot pins pierce the skin, no whips, no scalding tea,
Cheriffa and her spirits will rest well tonight.

Now by this lamp, one thousand nights, I'm bound to stay,
For he has pledged to keep me where I dwell tonight.
I wished for magic. And he? He granted stories,
So I settle on the task and say farewell, tonight.

As I, the Bard, am suddenly compelled to write,
One thousand poems more than I can tell tonight.

I am the Story

I am a living mythology, an ancient future,
Of legends unfolding. I am life evolving.
I am transformation, an amalgamation of change.
Is the mind in the body, or the body in the mind?
I am completely deranged, I am all seeing blind.

I am the salvation of restless humanity.
Not content, not consenting; I am polite profanity.
Broken chains of unicorn, I am the hunted and the horn.
I am the roaring lion, sleeping by your feet,
I found the stolen crown in the dragon's keep.

I am the dreamer of dreams,
Unfolding themes and song line streams.
Unpicking the seams of cultural leanings.
I am wide awake dreaming.

In the folly of futility, I am mutability.
Another narrative, A breathing dialogue,
I am the word, And the word Is
A bleeding monologue.

I am comic relief, the keeper of the peace,
I brought home the golden fleece.
I am the magician dancing with The Queen of Heaven.
Emptiness dancing. Asleep perchance to dream.

I'm a wizard, a sorceress, A bard, a druid.
I am timeless fluid. A button to press, or be pressed.
I'm unimpressed. Unconcerned by what I've learned.
I might be, I could be, I should be, I would be.

Nothing and everything matters to me.
Hallelujah! I am the story.

In Between.

It appears I am always in between,
somewhere I'm going
and somewhere I've been.

Between sunrise and sunset.
Between birth and death.
In the liminal Twilight,
where no one forgets.

Twixt the up and the down.
Twixt the in and the out.
In the liminal breath,
where no thing is found.

Between stillness and flowing.
Between stagnant and growing.
In the liminal landscape,
where no where is knowing.

Between sunset and sunrise.
Between Earth and sky.
In the liminal dawn,
where Awen resides.

It appears I am always in between,
somewhere I'm going
and somewhere I've been.

Peacock Breasted Waffle Muffin.

You peacock breasted waffle muffin
A wannabe pilgrim, temple quaffing,
Intolerant goatling of an Acolyte,
With the stench of sacred sanctified
In a dissociated mess of shrubbery.
You self-absorbed peddler of sorcery.

Wobbling down the street
With an AppleJack gait,
As if Captain Cockwomble
Married Judgy McJudgeface.
You hoary faced High Street stalker,
You felty fairy, barefoot walker.
You think you're mysterious and intense,
You're just a straggle haired witchwench.

A dithering dust monger,
A wretched faff of psychodrama,
A fluff headed fairy fancier,
And a gobby old God botherer.
A perambulating poetess,
Crumbling on an edifice of crisis,
As weak as these alliterated quips.
You faffing foolish fungalwhip!

Perhaps you think I am being rude,
To a bothersome Bard of ill repute,
But I am the Inner Critic,
I'm just a whimpering whelp,
And I can't quite get over
Being hard on myself.

Farewell

Give me another voice!
I want another poets words to grace the page.
Let us conspire, find another face to take the stage.
That's enough of my noise.

Give me a new rhythm!
Tales to trip on another tongue to twist myth and rhyme.
Someone new twixt muse and Awen shine
Let me hear that wisdom.

'Give me a fond farewell.'
I will remain a Bard after this initiation,
this a year and a day of pure inspiration.
I have older tales to tell.

REMNANTS OF A GIRL

Shadows on the Ceiling

There was a shadow of a rocking chair in the corner of the room.
It was high up on the ceiling and sometimes it would move.
No one tried to sit on it, there was nothing that could prove
It was even really there, but it was true.

There were cobwebs in the lampshade hanging heavy with the dust,
And sometimes I imagined the light played tricks and must
have cast a shadow on the corner of an empty rocking chair,
That wasn't really real, but it was there.

There was a suitcase on the wardrobe, folded blankets and some hats,
and every time I looked at them, I thought it might be that.
Throwing shapes on flaky paint, casting shadows in the cracks.
It wasn't really true, it was a fact.

There was a tree that tapped the window whenever the wind blew.
It reached up to the gutter and one night I just knew,
That the lightning and the thunder would soon reveal the truth.
Of the shadows that were playing in the roof.

There was lightning, there was thunder, there was power in the air,
And all the shadows came to me, invited me up there.
Lightning crackled, thunder growled, then things got really wild,
Upon my bedroom ceiling as a child.

Don't Say a Word.

As the branches I rest on are severed,
And I fall from the broken boughs.
Knowing the cradle can't hold me forever,
Falling, descending without a sound.

I shall never hear the mocking bird sing,
Before the coming of the flood.
I will never take that diamond ring,
And besides, it's soaked in blood.

The looking glass is smashed to bits,
And the billy goat won't pull.
The sturdy cart sits stubbornly,
Before a disillusioned bull.

The horse and hound have left the field,
To run wildly in the woods.
My sweet child's lips have been unsealed,
And finally I have understood.

Gifts, from birth to death's reaping,
Offered to the sweetest child in town,
Are foolish treasures not for the keeping,
And the cradle lies in pieces on the ground.

I am not flying, I'm falling with grace,
As the world seems to tear itself apart.
Don't be misled by the look on my face,
The sweetest gift of love is in my heart.

A Horrid Girl

There once was a girl,
And she had a little trouble
with a stupid little rhyme.
Who had a little curl,
and a man friend of her mum
would repeat it all the time.

Right in the middle of her forehead,
it drilled, setting metaphor
that did little to thrill her.
He found it delightful
when she was good,
and looked all demure,
like she found it funny,
or something other than frightful.

She was very very good,
at not letting on that it hurt her
as the terrible truth of it set in,
and when she was bad,
thinking of all the things she could do
if she was allowed to hurt him,
she was horrid.

When Good Friday Was Good

When I was just a rascal
with a cow licked curl,
ripping through concrete playgrounds,
and single mums had little time
for latch key kids like me,
Good Friday was good.

Moneylenders left their tables
and turned over profit
to go on holiday, while streets
retreated from hawking eyes.
Thoughts of Jesus chased off the traders,
And all the shops were empty.

Mum was home and King of her castle,
earned enough for a decadent weekend
with bacon for breakfast
and old movies for lunch.
But no eggs til Sunday,
so we crucified hot crossed buns for tea.

Me and my sister laughed
and conspired and we
sugar rushed to Sunday,
then competed for a month
to see who could make it last
the longest. Fragments snapped
and wrapped in gold.
A small sacrifice.

Little Donkey

I didn't want to be the star, or Mary,
I would have liked to be a King, but something was missing.
It was 1977, and we weren't that progressive.
The girls argued that a girl could be a shepherd,
and they were right, but Miss Shaeffer was having none of it.
Boys and tea towels, that's the tradition.

I could have been an angel, but there were only three
And even though I cried, it wasn't going to be me.
We could have all been angels, but the teacher said,
"with no one to carry the heavy load,
how would they make it to Bethlehem?"
Three kings, three shepherds, three angels, three sheep,
a star, a woman, a man, and a little donkey.

Little Donkey, little donkey on the dusty road.
That was me in the opening scene.
Through the school hall,
Behind an oversized mask,
In rubber soled pumps,
Covered in grey crepe paper,
careful not to hoof someone in the knee.

Got to keep on plodding onwards with your heavy load.
Through that sea of cross legged hecklers
Past the laughing and braying,
holding my head up high, and right behind me, Joseph and Mary.
Graceful past the boy who stuck out his leg to trip me.

That was when school still smelled waxy,
and giggles were innocence.
Before that tiny beast of burden knew
just what a heavy load entailed.
Before that Christmas Day.

Been a long time little donkey through the winter night.
War wasn't just in stories or movies, it was real.
Terror became a burden.

BETHLEHEM, Sunday, Dec. 25 1977
It was on the news,
On a tiny screen broadcast in black and white.
An explosion erupted last night
in a sidestreet off Manger Square,
where thousands of pilgrims celebrate.

Don't give up now little donkey, Bethlehem's in sight.
On Christmas Eve in the town of the birth of Jesus.
There were no reports of casualties among the throng in the square,
which was strung with Christmas lights and decorations.
"it's almost certain the explosion had come from a bomb."

Ring out those bells tonight Bethlehem, Bethlehem.
With innocence shattered,
Raining like broken glass in a sidestreet in Jerusalem.
I learned about Palestine and Israel and the war for peace.

Follow that star tonight, Bethlehem, Bethlehem.
Through snow screen and white noise,
Mum changed the channel to Judy Garland,
and the wicked witch of the West crushed and withered.
Oh, I would have gladly put on those red slippers.
There's no place like home. Curled up asleep in the armchair.

Little donkey, little donkey, had a heavy day.
The desecration of something sacred walked into my dreams.
The little Church in Bethlehem was whipped up into a tornado,
And the whole nativity swirled in the curls of the wild wind.
Angels, kings, shepherds and sheep,
A star, a woman, a man, saw the manifest glory
Of a 7 year old in a donkey mask,
Flying a bicycle in the blue, blue sky.

Little donkey, carry Mary safely on her way.
All the angels crowded round in paper wings and tinsel crowns,
The shepherds abandoned their crooks as sheep turned to clouds,
Wise men crowed about the right way to go.
No one else could see the star,
Because they had to look too far.
So they all followed the little donkey,
and the little donkey followed the star.

Little donkey, carry Mary safely on her way.
And somehow, against all reckoning, they all made it to the Manger.
But it wasn't Jerusalem any more, this stable stood alone.
A wooden nativity on the occasional table in the living room.

Follow that star tonight, Bethlehem, Bethlehem.
And beside the white tinsel Christmas tree,
Burdened with gifts of a hardworking mother's love,
Threads of silver over rainbow lights and bright red beads.
The little donkey put down her heavy load, climbed up on the table
and took the star from the top of the tree.

Bringing heaven to earth.
She stretched out beneath sparkling static,
And peered through the branches,
Looking for hope in the holy heart of home.

Smile Mona Pizza.

The most famous enigmatic smile,
Aligns with leaning towers,
And spicy pepperoni,
To conjure childish comedy.

A diminutive form,
Of a wicked nickname,
That everyone at school
Finds hilarious, but her.

Teasing out the meaning.
What is the Oath of God?
Mary's closest friend,
Who bore Holy John.

Queens and Mad hatters,
Depreciate her name.
Bets are off as mothers,
Inspired by popular media,
Fall to favour Graceland's daughter.

Simpsons sing a parody
Of happy birthdays,
Cat Stevens sees her sad.
Prince says she is nasty,
The King remembers her,
Long after he is gone.

Lou Reed, goes deep,
Wraps her in velvet,
Betrays her secrets and sings what she says!
No wonder everyone asks her to smile.

Woman noun; Adult Human Female

Don't you try to redefine me,
Don't you tell me what I am,
Don't tell my little girl,
That he's in the wrong body.

Don't clothe my tomboy in misconceptions
That something is wrong
Don't morph him into something else
while she searches for his place of belonging.

I sang my song through trials of femininity,
Of masculinity. Those days of 'Is it a he or a she?'
And, 'with a little bit of makeup, you would be so pretty.'
For me it was easy to see.

The fear of being a woman in this world.
Appeals to opposites, offering safety in dungarees,
To hide behind another gender.
I was just a child, jumping rooftops, climbing trees.

But, if they had redefined the meaning,
Of me, in case my tomboy was offended.
Had I been told a different story of
What I might or might not have been.

If my dysphoria had been upended,
In whispers of trans, or cis or terf,
For what it's worth, I ask myself,
Would I have changed my body or my mind?

Memory of a Girl

I wonder if some memories reside in the space that they were made,
echoes of distant times, remaining long after we have left the place.
Ghosts in the atmosphere of who we once were,
while we are still living, could a part of us still be there?

In northwest London, a brand new 70's construction
fourth floor, middle block, the hallway smelled of fresh emulsion.
A child, just seven years old, wilful, uncontrolled,
sent to her room, red faced and scolded.

Her sister was out, her mum was shouting
as she climbed the stairs, 13 of them. She was counting.
From under her sister's bed, where she ran and hid
among dusty sweet wrappers, her still shallow breath!

Just imagine staying there forever, among the lost treasures,
of childhood fantasy, living quietly on displeasure.
And discarded mouldy snacks, shifting right into the back,
disappearing into nothingness, leaving nothing there to smack.

Is she still there, now the tower blocks
have fallen into shallow gentrification,
Memory of a girl suspended,
high in the air of frightened anticipation?

Absent Hero

Wildest dreams of Silverstone, I saw you win the race.
Fist clouted air, but I never saw your face.
Brought champagne and flowers to a seven year old dream,
I know you came, you knew how much it would mean.

First mate upon your dream ship, a merchant vessel spent;
Swallowed the essence from a telegram you sent.
A box of cards to open in a teenage romance,
Tracing letters where I know your hand once danced.

I flew with you to Africa, saw zebras on the plain,
Real in colour father brought to life again.
With babe in arms, a mother, I looked and thought I saw,
A beaming grandpa peering through the door.

Now life without the hero who's eulogy I see.
Very much missed by wife, kids, grandchildren, and me.
Two lives you lived. The one you knew with wife and family,
And the one that I created and kept alive with me.

So, am I to mourn you? To kill the childhood dream.
Allow your death to tarnish my imagination's gleam?
No. I'll never say goodbye, since we never said hello.
Kinship passed us by like a wing of wicked crow.

I never can imagine you lying in a grave.
Nor deny your presence or the love you gave,
To bring this soul to being, to let me have my dream,
Of absent father hero, on whom my whole world leaned.

SHADES OF WOMAN

Girl, You are a Woman Now

How will you run
When the flood comes?
Life bears down,
Sore and tired,
Deep wounding.
And you realise,
there is blood on those lies.

Remember,
There is no 'away'
When the wolves
Come prowling.
Embracing wildness,
Forgiving the lack
Of teaching.
Girl, woman, mother soon.

Raw mystery.
A hundred thousand
Beating hearts
Encircle history.
The pulse before,
And the whisper after.
How do we run?

One after another.
Some run to find,
there is no 'away'.
Some remember to
'run with the wolves'.
We weren't taught how, we just ran!

Just One Bite

Somewhere between mythology,
a young woman's story
and someone's twisted version of reality.

She takes a bite of succulent delightful sin.
Breaking red skin,
revealing white flesh within.

She sinks to her knees as Genesis 3,
verse 16 spills its juice.
And she chews on her labours,

swallows her sorrows,
Not yet yielding to the will of another,
Learning from her mother's, mothers.

Truth or dare, she doesn't share.
Obviously!
No, not this one.

She ripens,
takes another bite of liberty.

Nothing Matters!

we strike out

like lunatics

tripping on

furtive corners

falling for starlight

and wild night's reason

lost in dazzled highs

where hunger

time and

distance become

insignificant

because

nothing

matters

but love.

City Lovers

I remember when
Love came fast
Like a hurricane,
And nothing mattered
But water,
And the distance home.

I remember when
Love lasted
There and back again,
And tripping starlight
Sparked a night
Eager with promise.

Conceived in concrete,
Love remained
While time slipped away
And the city streets
Remembered,
That we were lovers
full of hope.

I am Alive

Red light on Craven Park Road.
A scream not cried, drives into memory,
rainbow twist cord strangles the first breath
and leeches through time to stifle my energy.
Lights turn amber. I consider the haste
from birth to death, to be resurrected,
the cord untwisted, urged back to life.

I hold my breath. Imagine the rush
of garish blue lights, from the kitchen,
to ambulance medics and Royal Free
doctors. A mother, a baby revived,
survived, cheeks draining blue to blush.
Flashing lights a memory in my rear view.

Lights turn green. I change gear,
exhale, contract, tighten my grip,
wrestle my scarf away from my neck,
accelerate, and suppress a scream,
pull away from the street where I was born.

Later, walking past people
too scared to say good day.
I pull myself in and fade to grey.
Make of me a shadow, to not offend life
and hide behind skilful detached illusion.

Black lipped and stifled in the city
I was born in. A billboard jolts me
from choking and I draw a sharp breath,
when it lights up and shouts out loud.
'Are you alive!?' And I know,
I'm not dead yet.

A Portrait Hides a Thousand Lies

She draws lines of joy around her eyes
to disguise sorrow,
paints a picture of tranquility
to nurture grace,
makes crude stick figures
of a brighter tomorrow,
and colours in the best bits,
the bits that keep her safe.
Sometimes she dreams of Micheal Finnegan,
wishes she could tear it up and begin again.

She once drew a windmill
to chew up all the grist,
her face shows the creases
of sweet memories and sadness,
She hides her power in a chain
clasping her elegant wrist,
subtle charms of a life well lived.
Sometimes she dreams of wonder woman,
wishes she could spin around and make it alright again.

She remembers sun filled days on the beach,
warmer days of cuddles and love,
grasping way beyond her reach,
of thinking she was good enough.
She paints an enigmatic smile on her lips,
and behind her lies a secret,
that she lived, and loved, and lost,
just like all the rest,
and while she may not be perfect,
she did her very best.
Sometimes she dreams of the ducks on the bank,
wishing the water would roll off her back.

Shake off the Folly

Shake off the folly of trying to make it,
Take off the shame of trying to fake it,
Trade off the part you persist to partake in,
Remake a world you want to awake in.

Turn off the light so you can see clearly,
Step up to embrace and enter the black,
Take a walk in the darkness to find your clarity,
Enter the labyrinth, bring yourself back.

Explore the places you have hidden the key to,
Take up the shadows like an old linen sheets,
The promises broken, the power you yield to,
Shake out those dusty old memories of weakness.

Remember those times that you found it, or lost it,
Shake off your delusion; there's nothing inside.
Send skeletons scattering out from the closet,
Take a good look at what your mind tries to hide.

In the deepest darkest place in the story,
The inner world where you govern yourself,
Where no one is seeking Hail, Grail or Glory,
A warrior stalks in spite of her stealth.

Shake off the folly of trying to make it,
Take off the shame of trying to fake it,
Trade off the part you persist to partake in,
Remake a world you want to awake in.

Witch Woman?

Left naked and fearful,
Stripped bare with no footfall.
Ripped apart until the you
You knew is not the you
You thought you knew.

She will pursue you,
And eat away everything.
Until all you are left with is
A spark of fire in the noise.
An expression of divinity,
With fire in your voice.

Women like her, once were revered,
The mystics, prophets and witches.
Loved before they were feared,
turned into crones and bitches.

They were seen as distinguished
and powerful then.
Before they were diminished,
by giants and small minded men.

She's not belittled by the twisting of myths,
She knows where she came from.
She knows who she is.
She is primal, powerful and sure in her surety.

No need to shout her glory.
There's only one story.
Women of power, women who know it,
Quietly live out their own mythology.

Crone

Newborn eyes to absorb the world,
Growing, wild eyes of knowing.
She's a long way from there.
Wonder filled stare.
Things were different then.
Did she know that?
These days hold less gifts,
more promise.
Age would change her.

She's travelled unseen,
seeking promises in the dark.
Knowing pain to dance with fear.
In with a cord suppressing her scream,
until she birthed - full of her self,
let her voice free to howl at the world.
She is not what she seems.

Dreams of worn memory
begot a tale of growing old.
Wrinkles of time to taint her skin,
spots of age on the hand to find
a picture tucked in a purse.
Unfolded, creases smoothed, soothed.

Held, throughout existence.
Baby kept safe in a sepia pose.
An image reflects what was, to what is.
Baby, girl, maiden,
warrior, woman, lover,
mother, elder, crone.
Welcome Home.

ECHOES OF FAMILY

Can't Sleep at Mother's House

The clock ticks too loud.
Yet light fades, gives way to night.
I can't sleep at mother's house
Curtains cotton thin, let the street lights in.
Time passing,

Shaded memories, awake when you go to bed.
There in the corner, a wall of VHS,
A dusty, grainy monumental waste,
a taste of remembrance of shared time.
Time passing,

There in the shadow, a dictionary.
Old words I used to search for,
Lost to us by now, replaced with
cyber references she doesn't understand.
Time passing,

That candlestick, a Christmas gift,
the one I made for her in 1986.
Azure glass glaze, my fingerprints
Remain forever in the clay.
Time passing,

Traces of a teenager, in remembrance.
I remember when I had that party
and the neighbour grassed on me,
She didn't like her, but misses her, now she's gone.
Time passes,
the clock ticks too loud.

A Picture Paints a Family

Who could see it in that picture
Of us standing on the beach?
The goals that we would score
And the dreams we'd fail to reach?

Dressed all in our finest,
Shabby from head to toe.
Don't judge us on that premise,
It was chic and just for show.

See the effort of the eldest,
In the tightness of her hand?
Restrained from making rabbit ears
While smiling on demand.

Could we ever understand
The challenge for her brother?
Contained for a whole four seconds
While being shot, stifled and smothered.

And posing there behind him,
The shyest of all the kids,
Her coyness covers confidence
And a wildness kept well hid.

And, oh so cute, the youngest
Is raising just one eyebrow,
For the future us to notice
The sparkle in his scowl.

Yes, dad and I look frazzled,
Innocent and young,
Before we knew the majesty
Of the beauty yet to come.

Oh, how the years have changed us all
From a dusty family portrait,
To living dreams and heroes
Hiding in plain sight.

A picture paints a thousand dreams,
Of excited expectation,
But who can tell what dreams are real,
And what are fabrications?

Haunted by Berry Pomeroy

Where sun parched fields meet
shadows of emerald kissed hollows,
blanched trees climb a too high horizon
and dusty lichen smacks the air.

Where rhododendron, not native,
Invader roots in Devon's red earth. Immature,
hard and green in the bountiful hedgerow
among ripening seed heads and rosing hips.

.

Dad leads the way. Her, too teenage,
scuffs plimsolls in the dust and falls behind.
Nurtured by the hollow that hems her in.
She alone sees the heartsease, blooms fading.

Sulking past old barns, a derelict mill,
a fungus fort grown on an old tree stump.
Her brother makes up an everyday miracle.
Dad mocks a noisy fight with an invisible boar.

He nearly makes her laugh.
Set on a mission to find the ruins of Berry Pomeroy,
Dad swaps from adventurer to teacher,
trips back in time to tales of a Norman Conquest.

She races to St Margaret's tower, steals a glance
through the barred window where Eleanor's jealousy
imprisoned her own sister to starve to death.
Maybe the birds stop singing.

Her little sister finds the wishing tree first.
Counts copper dreams turning green with age,
old desires cushioned in moss. Dad winks,
offers her a penny; she's still good for wishing.

An Unbroken Minute of Silence

An unbroken minute of silence,
echoes remembrance and loss.
Still warriors are sent to fight,
while nations count the cost.

A banner cries 'Never Again!'
A white poppy wreath flecked with red,
reminds us why we remember,
the servicemen lying dead.

The comrades who never,
come home to our arms.
The soldiers; broken warriors,
no longer tend the farm.

The medals in their boxes,
the names we won't forget.
The distant graves unvisited,
grandfathers we never met.

Do they still die for you and me?
do they die to continue the violence?
Do they die so that we can remember in
an unbroken minute of silence?

Stirring the Sky

Everyday I saw that portrait of you,
Smiling like a movie star.
Mum sat it by the front door,
I wanted to remember you young.
To know you when you met him,
See how your cheeks flushed,
When he kissed them.
All I could see was monochrome.

Shiny boots and flying jacket,
The softness of his collar.
When you nestled your head
Into his shoulder.
Did you find comfort there,
Before he left?
If you knew he wouldn't return,
Would you have let him go?

What choice is there?
When eagles on buttons
Are a cold call of duty
To Crown and country.
How could you not know,
When he learnt how to fly?

He would forever be stirring the sky.
His life, a hero, sacrificed,
To a monochrome movie,
Played every anniversary.
So I could imagine the man
My grandfather might have been.

After Me the Flood

617 Squadron remembered on a roundel.
A plain wall fractured by three flashes of lightning.
From the breach, water rapids.
Aprés moi, le déluge.

Operation chastise. The dams busted up,
Water swirling down takes out the power ops.
The water engulfs a train with passengers.
After me the flood.

A wing shears past with a violent patch of flak.
Burpee acts fast, dives away from the attack.
Billy hits em back, fire sears the sky.
German gunners flank, we're hit! We fall, we die.
Aprés moi, le déluge.

Left a box of medals, a cracked photograph,
A telegram, single mother, and a distant epitaph.

And we never forget,
Watch The Dambusters year after year.
Sit in silence while mother remembers,
Our grandmother's tears.
After me, the flood.

Intangible Chaos

Hear in the silence,

        of unfolded clothes

and creased up linen,

        last night's dinner

smells in the kitchen,

        washing up stacked

to topple and drop,

        dusty old corners

hiding lost socks,

        damp towels in the bathroom,

and empty loo rolls,

        grimy bathtub,

hair blocked plug hole,

        a crack in the paintwork,

the dent on the floor,

        crumbs round the toaster,

leaves by the door.

Hear in the chaos
of storm before calm.
Nobody means any harm.

Don't Cross That Line!

'Don't cross that line.' I said, and he didn't.
He walked right on it. Balanced on the,
bounds of limitation, at the edge of crisis.

Teetering on whitelines on the platform,
protection from the trains buffeting.
He was only three, already liberated.

Walking the line. Free to topple,
one side or the other, to safety, or to danger.
Then the train came.

My hand held back,
from grabbing him,
my heart like,
mortar in my breast.
Trust.
The wild wind,
thrust against his body.
Trust.
The raw adventure in his blue eyes.
He doesn't want to colour in the lines.

Trust.
Watch him shine.
Celebrate his wildness,
show him where the line is,
and know he will draw his own.
Lines that define his wild nature,
boundaries that he can be within.
Not a mother's cotton wool
smothered love;
Trust.

Rummaging for Marbles.

I will always love my junk drawer,
All the items that remain,
To serve as a reminder,
Every step of the way.

There are lids to fit boxes,
That don't even exist,
So my love can't be contained,
In a wish for all I wish.

Half burnt birthday candles,
Kept for future usefulness,
Light shines in the darkness,
Wish for joy and happiness.

Broken LED lights,
Missing buttons and dead batteries,
Symbolic of the sacrifice,
Of all I've ever dreamed.

Another thing that stays with me,
Is relentless Mr Blender,
Pushing on through thick and thin,
A powerful reminder.

Salty sachets of remembrance,
Sauce to serve, in times of lack,
Conjure up preparedness,
And keeping something back.

I fumble through these memories,
I hope life treats me kind,
And that I can find my marbles,
When I start to lose my mind.

Foolish Cat

The best cat we ever had,
Alfie, eternal fool,
Crossed the road on
All Fools Day, before midday.

All that's left is
a whisker on the mat.
Black and white hairs
on my jacket, Where he napped.

The haunting fact,
His absence in the garden,
Magpie's relief.
A world turned monochrome,
Rolled over and stained red.

Across the road a sign said,
'A361 Lighten the Load'.
It was April Fools.

I wished it was a joke.

Magnificat

Primary chief familiar am I to the Goodwins.
And my native country is Glastonbury.
Max the Wizard called me Alfie,
But all future humans shall call me Magnificat.
I was nine full months in the alleyways of Axminster.
Before that I was Charlie, but now I am Magnificat.

I was a rider of the Wirral Hill dragon
When the Holy Thorn fell to chainsaw.
I carried the rabbit before Gingerninja.
I know the names of the stones
From The Dragon Hill to the River Brue.
I was in the bender when Kath was well.
I was on the lap before the birth of Lyla.

I was a destroyer to the slow worm.
I shall be a curl of smoke around your legs.
I was patriarch to kittens and kittens.
Before I was snipped. I was there at the destruction
Of the neighbour's wild garden.
I was in Roman Way before we moved to town.

I came here to the remnant of Bere Lane.
I rolled around in the manger cleaning my ass.
I swirled leaves through water in a puddle.
I was at the crossroads with the bards.
I was the muse from Lisa's cauldron.

I was stretched out in the sun in nonchalant mindfulness.
I shall be as the Night Jasmine on the face of the fence.
I sat on the bardic chair. I have crossed the perilous road
To the Abbey. I shall continue to revolve
Between the three black dots on my nose.

A Whisper of your Ancestor

Existence comes bounding;
And roaring through creation.
Resounding over vines of time.
On every breath, a whisper.

They come riding on atoms and
Bear fruit.
They conspired and begot me,
To travel along these lines of infinity.

Manifested my glory from the,
Divine expression of ancestry.
Giant shoulder to giant shoulder,
Their power to stand upon.

Laying down their blood and bone;
Foundations set for storyline.
Living mythology in the
Root of our bloodlines.

Oh, hundreds came before me!
All those lives that collided to create me,
Love making lines in the webs of time,
Love made real by their design.

And when I lay down my bones,
Onto the timeless tale of descent,
My love will leave a sweet story.
My blood will bleed generations.

And I will journey on to be,
A shoulder for the rest to rest upon.
I will ride on the breath and you will hear,
A whisper of your ancestor.

Rebel Teacher

Kids in Chaos

The Educational Psychologist puts it in context,
To a room full of teachers, he defines the problem,
Of children, disordered and unruly,
I raise my hand,
'Please Sir – would you have judged me so shrewdly?'

What would you have seen in that kooky, choosy, screwy,
fruity, moody, loony teen?
What would you have got if you put me in a box,
Tried to unlock the paradox of that disruptive chatterbox?

A genius with Aspergers or ADHD?
Oppositional defiant with a conduct disability,
A strong willed drama diva with 'how to behave' amnesia.

Each day I went home with a general adaptation syndrome,
And a touch of hyper-mania. It gets even more insania.
Little impulse control, malingering manic episodes,
Post traumatic embitterment, Rationally belligerent,
Seasonal adjustment, rebellion ... deliberate.

Would you have had the time or inclination to define,
The child who wouldn't conform to society's conditioned norm?

Would you make a box to put me in?
Chuck me in the water to sink or swim?
Would you write my statistics down while I drown or clown around?

Would I get a bitter pill to still the stress
of not being what you expect;
the kind of child selected, to be the perfect prefect,
Too numb to be anything but an invisible defect.

Sitting still in class – ification,
Hiding my irrepressible rebellion,
Just in case you try to kill my spirit with a regularly taken pill.

And would your pill find me somewhere to be real?
Someone to see beneath the skin, would it keep the pain in?
So it don't spill in the halls and run down the walls,
soaking my playground fears in tears of public rain.
Can a pill kill that pain? Please, assess and test me again.

Would I think you were wise as the spark leaves my eyes,
And my genius dies while you sit in your suit and itemise
My disorder that's leaving every cell in my being
screaming 'I'm sorry I'm me.' I felt free!
I thought I could be who I wanted to be.

I was too unconventional, I did things unmentionable,
I was too objectionable, and not at all 'sit on that bench!' able.
Would you make me broken and rein me in,
take the credit for fixing me with a dose of Ritalin?

Kids too fast, kids too slow,
those who don't know where to go.
Kids too cheeky, kids too sneaky,
those too challenging, or just a bit peaky.
Kids too truthful, kids too rue-full,
those too 'won't follow what you do!' full.
Kids too contentious, kids too rebellious,
those opting out of the prospectus of correctness.

Is it right to dull the zealous and impetuous?
The marvellous and rebellious,
Discontented, disaffected, yet connected?
How do you decide who's respected or rejected?

Kids in chaos. A common disorder,
Not being what society thinks you oughta.

Education Other Wise

We are taught to believe that education is compulsory.
But it's not the forced conscription that they make it out to be.
The pre-programmed prescription of a sick society,
That teaches me to forget that the choice is down to me.

Soon children will be taught to work a ten hour day,
With sixty quid fines if you take them on a holiday.
If they taught us how to manage money maybe we could pay,
For our children Not to face those bullies every day.

For them Not to endure the regular playground destruction,
That happens everyday with no resilience instruction.
And to not StandUnder the authoritarian functions,
Of, 'do your best, toe the line and be fearful of sanctions.'

Decide at thirteen what you wanna be when you're older.
Be a good little girl or a brave little soldier.
And never, ever, ever forget what we told ya;
Don't you try to be special or anything bolder.

How does it work when my ideas are bigger than me,
But my brilliance doesn't come from a GCSE?
When education is a privilege and it's offered for free,
Yet we nurture in a culture of low self esteem.

When all those resources are forced on those poor kids.
They lose the respect of the forces that force it.
Low attendance reports are enforcing a lawsuit,
With financial sanctions and we just can't afford it!

Is the knife in the back, or the back on the knife?
When all we really need to teach is a way to feel alive
I'll meet you on the other side of Education.
At school or OtherWise.

Exceptional Circumstances

"Absence Will Only be Authorised in Exceptional Circumstances!"
Unusual, like a family death or serious illness,
Not typical, like dawn at Stonehenge on Summer Solstice,
Uncommon, like a parental access visit abroad,
Atypical, like going to a famous fairy ball.

Extraordinary, like a child who is autistic,
Out of the ordinary, like a trip on a spaceship,
Unexpected, at the discretion of the parents,
Unprecedented, mental distress under a Tory government.

Exceptional, disability or distress or fright,
Outstanding, disorder or the need for family respite,
Rare, like winning a holiday as a prize,
Peculiar, like living on the Isle of Wight.

Bizarre, like a close to home bereavement,
Inconsistent, work requirements of parents,
Odd, when Family Fund makes awards for family holidays,
Weird, the amount won't cover allowed peak season holidays.

Non-standard, a school trusting a parent's judgement,
Freaky, working travellers, performers and showmen,
Divergent, experience of family culture and heritage,
Last chance, visiting an old or sick relative.

Irregular, like family weddings, christenings, and funerals,
Strange, like different term dates for children in different schools,
Deviant, parents in charge of their children, not the state,
Surprising, like the chance to join a thrilling pirate raid.

Of course, this list is exceptional, we are living in exceptional times,
It's unusual, not typical, to allow enough time for family time.
Would you go AWOL for circumstances such as these?

Results Day - You Passed

A star!
Be clever and
C the way to
Define the worth of
Each person
oF distinction.
U made it!
Congratulations!
Kid, you got results!

I hope you got what you needed from whatever the State provided,
That replication of information they decided to call education.
Whether you shone or whether you hid, amid the limitations.
However you didn't do or did, despite the expectations.
Whatever the A,B,C of who is better than me.

The sum of all those years, of coping with the fears,
And emotional equations of complications at school.
Trying your best to be seen to follow the rules,
While suffering fools. Gladly or badly.
Trying to sit still, keep your cool.

However they scored you;
That mark on the paper,
To specify whether you are stupid or clever.
Know this; You passed!
Oh Yes! You passed.
All the shoulder barges,
All the knocks and hardships.
The name calling and uniform rules.
The blisters you got from new school shoes.
All the expectations and unfounded limitations.

Through silent inner breakdowns
In staged assembly breakthroughs,
Through all the lies and the truths.

All the not being heard
Because you're only a youth.

You passed!
You made it!
You Aced it!

Yes, even if you didn't stick around to face it,
And you were forced to choose
to find another way through.
And learn in a way that suits you.

Yeah, you Aced it too.

Those mindful of the Peace of avoiding the Queues,
Those who crossed their eyes and spotted the Tease.

You see; Genius isn't in a GCSE;
We are fabulous and unique,
Nurturing A Level of brilliance,
That no one could ever see,
From looking at your A,B, C's
Defined in a score on a sheet.

So whatever the number or letter,
And despite the contradiction,
Know that you did so much better!
And that's a worthy Distinction.

'Made Up' Workshops

We pride ourselves on the quality of our 'Made Up' classes.
100% guarantee you will be 'Made Up' at the results.
Click here to see a list of our most popular
'Made Up' workshops.
Special offer on The Present Moment!
Sign up for more details.

I'm gonna get enlightenment, I'm gonna run a class,
Your spiritual revival, a quick fix to last,
Smoke screen remover, ego massage,
A name retrieval, transflamation class,

Anxiety teaser, super tantric blast,
Trauma releaser, have the last laugh,
Toe in the water, head out of your arse
Manage your anger, for an hour and a half,

Become a believer, step out of the dark,
Nothing deceives ya, get enlightenment fast.
Sign up for a 'Made Up' workshop today!
Special price just for you!

*Small print; honestly, don't bother reading it, it's not important enough to be bigger
and it absolves us of any requirements to deliver anything at all. This is a piss take.
'Made Up' classes are for entertainment purposes only and have no direct benefit at all.
Classes subject to extortionate fees and a lot of time and effort on your part. No
responsibility or accountability can be placed on facilitator or facilitation. If you get
nothing out of it it is probably because you put nothing in, you ungrateful sod, try
taking charge of your life instead of placing your faith in some kind of Made Up
noo-nah.*

*DISCLAIMER. I am in fact an excellent teacher and workshop leader. I teach
firewalking and offer quality classes as well as directing a comprehensive syllabus and
membership group online at Wizards of Avalon. www.wizardsofavalon.com*

SHAPES OF A POET

Just a Little Poem

I'm just a lonely poem
sat here on my own,
not the kind of poem
that everybody knows.

I'm just a little riff
and you might have realised,
I'm not as wise as If,
you don't see me, Still I Rise.

I don't wander Lonely as a Cloud
or Compare You to a Summer's Day.
I won't make a generation Howl,
I'll just Go Gently on my way.

I don't mind if I'm not noticed
or if you pass me by.
I'm just an isolated poem,
Left here to make you smile.

Ruba'i Time

Tick and tock, and in between the silence,
It's volume stalks those ageing in defiance,
And cuckoo marks the passing of the hour,
As age survives no fleeting faith or science.

The scent of dust will drift on through the ages,
As cool aroma fills an old book's pages.
None can escape the passing of it's fragrance,
Familiar odours, memory exchanges.

And it is not so easy on the eye,
As blossom falls to mark it passing by,
A youthful face will gaze upon the mirror,
To see the creases in it glorified.

Although the minutes and the hours pass,
We may count them with each finger's touch,
Yet shifting changes nobody can grasp,
Our bones will feel its bold relentless march.

Villanelle for a Journalist

I can't decide between the pen and sword,
when terror is a weapon; all a fright.
A tempered blade is sharper than the word.

When blood is splattered on the storyboard,
and murder culls the freedom to incite,
I can't decide between the pen and sword.

When murder comes to call, it's quite absurd;
religion is afforded so much might.
A tempered blade is sharper than the word.

When guillotine is rust and fear re-stored,
and justice calls the body to the fight,
I can't decide between the pen and sword.

If I should write until my pen is purged,
would ink and paper, history rewrite?
A tempered blade is sharper than the word.

Oh, I would break the chains and cut the cord!
And if I need a weapon for that fight,
I can't decide between the pen and sword.
A tempered blade is sharper than the word.

Workers Sonnet

There is a fire burning without smoke.
Fed not by wood, but cold austerity
and burning embers will not be provoked
by wishful thinking, hope or charity.

For now the workers rights have all been sold.
The welfare state has undergone reform,
and all the skilled are sick or on the dole,
to find an occupation filling forms.

When people feel their purpose turn to dust
and suicide becomes their discontent,
for them to rest in peace, we simply must,
pick up the pace and pulse of dissidence.

So we will forge a fire in their name.
Bring branches of dissent to feed the flame!

Shall I Compare a Sonnet?

Shall I compare thee, laughter, light and love,
to expectations of the common man?
Is water, food and shelter not enough,
to make us feel we're dealt a decent hand?

To all those seekers, reaching for the light,
who grasp the shadow of the early morn.
Who, waking hungry from eternal night,
then face the rising of a daily storm.

Know is it safe to sit amidst the shade.
To witness all the damage that's been done.
To hold the darkness, then to feel embraced,
By gems of truth that never seek the sun.
Can love and light and laughter then remain,
when what we hide in shadows is betrayed?

Cinquain Ship

A song
seems so contrived
when asked to sit in line,
with certain tone and certain beat,
Retreats.

The words
will hit the page,
like regimented men,
to march through thought and back again,
to build

A cage
to hold the word,
to tame the urgent beast,
with artistic, rigid word-smith,
Release

The muse
to break the bind,
I place upon my mind.
Less fear that it's not good enough,
to speak

The truth
may never fit
the limited constraint,
The reins of time and rhyme and beat,
and when

I
let
the
word
splash
on a textile
of perception
with magnificent
certain deception
and expression
of shape
Rebel.

Resist
The cinquain ship
Of 2, 4, 6 ,8, 2,
One stressed, one unstressed syllable
To count.

To learn,
And try once more,
To fit the fated form,
I take myself to the water
and drown.

Splutter,
Capture accent,
Emotion on the wind,
I am grasping for a cliché!
Rescind.

AWEN,
Inspiration,
Takes pleasure in my pain,
As the stress of stresses takes me
Again.

Reader,
Can I ask you
To stop and take a count
Of the syllables and accent
of stress?

or
drop
into the
wide ocean
of word and cliché
let me be your mirror
wandering through the clouds of dreams on streams of lovliness
pouring forth out of the human mind, mankind faking then
shaking and awakening all kinds of forms and shape
shifting, smoke lifting in sublime rhyme
chaotic form where nobody knows
the prose where no-one was
taught how to dance a
stanza with
grace
truth comes
from another place
dancing unfettered magic
and a dreamer's magical action
picks up pen and paper and lends his hands
free and simple and under no bounds to the sound
of his grounded truth no grammar can bind no punctuation blind
the simplicity and essence
of a star who shines
in truthful
word
and
I

Waka Tanka

Okay! I will write.
Another bloody poem,
within a structure.
My frustration is owing,
to my need to make it flow.

Writing a poem
in 17 syllables,
is very diffi.
Cult japanese poetry,
gives me more verbosity.

So I take my time,
and when I try a haiku;
try to make it rhyme.
I find I need an extra,
few syllable and lines

When I look for words,
for to fit into this form.
Like swift hummingbird
another poem is born.
My love for word is absurd!

Really? do I need
to use classic japanese
to say what I mean?
Hear this analyses
on waka tanka I lean.

And my mind drifts off,
to cherry blossom and love,
sushi and saki,
and technology and stuff,
but I know that's not enough.

And 5, 7, 5,
with extra 7, 7,
is much more alive.
But maybe an 11,
is a more exquisite way to word heaven.

If You Can Keep Your Head when all about you are losing theirs, you have probably underestimated the situation.

What if you trust yourself, although you're doubted,
What if you wait, and wait, and wait again for nowt,
What if lies are not just told, but they are flouted,
What if haters hating turns into a clout?

What if you look fantastic and talk wise,
What if no one wants to listen to your voice,
What if your fate is written in the skies,
What if you get lost in all the fucking noise?

What if dreaming passes by while life moves faster,
What if thinking just becomes a daily bane,
What if you made friends with triumph and disaster,
And other friends with not so subtle names?

What if your tender heart is raw and breaking,
What if you only pledge to speak the truth,
What if silence licks your throat when you are speaking,
What if words are stuck behind a wall of wounds?

What if every day you feel like you are winning,
Turns into two more days you're bound to lose,
And every day begins a new beginning,
Of all the other things you failed to choose?

What if this poem's wisdom is found wanting,
To throw a tantrum, pack it's bags and shift,
What if we could all be still amid the ranting,
What if we would stop our asking... Oh, what if?

With all the shit and shine and shadow hunting,
This life we have been given is a gift.

Reluctant Priestess

For the Love of It!

Propped up on priestess pedestal of someone else's creation.
In disgrace to fall, a human declination.
Down in the gutter where the water runs white,
And many people mutter, judging wrong or right.
Throw off the ugly duckling and swim like static swan,
Furiously paddling beneath the gracefully done.

There's a goblin in the garden, he's shouting all the day.
I try to sit and listen to what he's got to say,
If he gets the time he needs, we might have a peaceful day,
But if he gets abusive, I'll have to send him on his way.

Answer all the questions. Do you know the way to the Tor?
"Wellhouse built 18 lickety split," like I've never said it before.
A loving family drops by, a woman claims liberation,
Wonder full in children's eyes, restored by restoration.

A wounded fellow hurt my pride, he tried to steal my fire,
My warmth will never be denied, passion's a blaze to inspire.
See, I cannot be stolen from, for I do freely give.
For the love of every one. For the love of It.

To sup from poisoned chalice or sip from holy cup.
Whatever way you drink it the core value is Love.

I Want to Move to Glastonbury

I want to move to Glastonbury!
I'd climb the Tor every day.
I want to move to Glastonbury,
To live my life in an 'Oh so spiritual way.'

I want to move to Glastonbury,
I would get up with the dawn;
Do yoga in the morning before
I get a chance to yawn.

I want to move to Glastonbury,
I could move into an Ashram,
I want to move to Glastonbury
Start every day with bhajans.

I want to move to Glastonbury,
Open a self-help book emporium.
Be a famous Avalonian,
Be a pseudo-historian.

A sustainable, ethical business-woman,
Make eco-friendly lotions and potions.
I will deal with my demons!
I'll handle my emotions!

I want to move to Glastonbury,
To hang out with the hippies,
Meet the Druids, be a Bard;
Write poems and folkish ditties.

I want to move to Glastonbury,
Do tarot at the Spring,
Go shopping for incense at Star Child,
Wearing my finest, glitter, fairy wings.

I want to move to Glastonbury,
Wear purple velvet dresses,
Put flowers in my hair;
Be really abundant and totally blessed.

I want to be the priestess.
The Goddess loves the bestest,
I want to be enlightened
Like all the rest .... Is.

I want to move to Glastonbury.
Oh ... you've heard it all before?
But I want to move to Glastonbury,
To fix that problem under the Tor.

I want to move to Glastonbury,
To heal the Holy Thorn.
I'll change my name to Crystal Clear
And I will be Reborn!

I want to move to Glastonbury,
Have tea with new age gurus,
I want to open a raw food deli,
Study cabala, practice voodoo, hoodoo, you do,

I'm gonna teach the healing that you do.
I'll have colonic irrigation,
And deal with all the doo doo.

I want to move to Glastonbury
Be a Wiccan Hindu Buddhist
I'm gonna be very grounded
in Avalon's holy mist.

I want to move to Glastonbury,
But everybody knows,
You can't just move to Glastonbury,
Only the chosen get to go.

And then it happened,
I got to move to Glastonbury.
I'm a lucky lucky thing!
To sip from golden chalice,
And sit by holy springs.

I got to move to Glastonbury.
Oh, it made my heart sing
And here my friends,
Is where the trouble begins.

I got to move to Glastonbury,
It was a tricky start,
Yet, there I found community,
To really warm your heart.

I was free to be me,
I could dress how I please.
I could fill my bucket,
With a truckle of cheese.

I could love and get loved up,
Do rituals for the bees,
I could step into my power,
And everyone could see!

Then the mill began to turn,
And so the rumours started,
Someone said I summoned demons,
every time I farted!

Next thing I'm a witch.
(I'm supposed to feel offended?)
Which is pretty kitsch,
So I wasn't upended.

He said, "You do black magic,"
I said, "Sir, you're a fool!"
Oh, I tried to keep my patience.
But I fear I lost my cool,
and I wasn't feeling so spiritual.

I got to move to Glastonbury,
Now I'm screaming on the High Street,
Cos some nutter's pissed me off,
And I couldn't give a hundred monkey's
What anybody thinks!

I got to move to Glastonbury
And so started the gnosis.
I got to have a soiree
And a dance with my psychosis.

And everyone but me can see,
Where the bogey on my nose is
While I get lost in the process of,
Process, process, process!

Process, surrender, fucking process,
Process, process – what the fuck! Process,
Process, surrender, process.
Surrender to the process.

I got to move to goldfish bowl,
Where I couldn't stub my toe,
Wipe my arse or blow my nose
without everybody knowing.

In the open air asylum,
the cracks, they started showing,
Like embracing the siren,
There's no escape, no going.

And before I knew what I was hiding
I discovered what I'm showing.
And thus began the process of truly growing.

Darkness Beckons

On the threshold into blackness,
Hear the waters, smell incense on the air,
Darkness beckons – dare.

Vast cavern, embracing chamber,
Candlelight ripples, pools of consciousness,
Pathways to providence. Deep in the well.
Where mystery dwells, follow the track,
Flips under, over and back.

Into the gateway, otherworld bidding,
Time shifting altar, Seasons of day to day,
The King of the Realm of Fae,
Wildwood Lord, strength of stag,
Graceful yielding to treasure within,
The heartbeat of Gwyn.

Upstream, a salmon's leap, calls deeper, deeper,
Living hazel bower, hold Brigit's Fire
To incite, inflame, desire.
Flame of Divine consciousness,
Alights upon the brow,
The time is now.

The waters pull, impassioned call,
Deep dark cauldron. Our Lady of Avalon,
Waters of purification,
Dive the depth of spirit, breath leaves body,
Sensation, purity, creation, embody.
Embrace the dark, then embark into the sun.
Dismembered are remembered.
Become one.

Loving Well

A heart is held enthralled by stone and water,
It's beating pulse is fed by constant flow,
In face of threat or danger, it won't falter
And even when disaster bucks the bow.

Once, twice, thrice, by strife, a love is tested,
This love requires utter sacrifice,
Lay down my self, my life, at once invested,
Embraced and held by otherworldly sighs.

Defying definition, Oh my love,
To make of me the novice, and the brave.
Release all inhibition, not enough!
To walk into the darkness of the cave.

Living on the edge of a cold chasm,
Allowed to put the grapes upon the vine,
Driven by an archetypal passion,
Swallowed by the taste of love divine.

And hidden in the shadow cast by candles,
A heart trips on the strings of pure delight,
And bidden by the hallows of the deep well,
It brings a loving presence to the light.

Gateway to the Otherworld

She stands there at the border,
Fears the rawness and the power, still.
Hears the splash of steel on water,
'Neath a famous tower on a hill.

Bruises excite the sky outside,
Beads of blood dry on the yew.
A yapping dog laps at the water,
A chestnut mare clips at the dew.

She goes barefoot in ice cold water.
Gazing through black iron curves,
Blue lias stone and wet lime mortar,
Affirms to The Lady, "May we never thirst!"

Alerted, a red breasted robin,
Alights a staircase of marble, white.
Beyond a stone hall, she imagined,
A glorious garden in the moonlight.

A place of fae, where some are sweet
And some are troublesome; hellish,
Some are tempted by a naked treat,
Others are richly embellished.

Hand written, a paper prayer on violet,
Carried on the wings of a swan,
For the love of Culhwch and Olwen.
A wish on the way to the old ones.

Carved crystal is blushed by the silt,
Of years in the roots of the place.
Now nothing is sold; the export is love.
Now, no one is charged, and no one is paid.

For the Love of It – Whatever It is.
The raw concentration of life,
Himself, the lover of Crythyladd,
For Him. For Her. There is no price.

Outside the windows, we see back inside
An ancient treasure remembered.
Find a little bit of eternity,
In a love so purely tended.

Note to Destruction

Under the full moon and crashing storms,
Mighty doors and lashings torn,
By wild winds and emotion.
What a test of my devotion!

Am I to crumble in the debris
Left by your madness or hubris?
Do you wish me to lay it to waste,
Give in and board up the place,
That I love?

No, I am so much stronger than before,
You came and smashed down the doors.
Yes, I am strengthened by your weakness,
Does that make me anything less?

I wish you no harm or retribution from karma.
I know it is so much harder for you to redress your own
Brokenness than it is for me to put right this mess.

See, to me this is just another test,
And you call in your own justice.
So I will remove the splinters,
Pick up the pain of your mental distress.

I will turn this around and
Continue to be unstoppable.
And you will see,
Another world is possible.

A Wyrd Conversation with The Sky

The night sky, clad in star light, stepped forth.
Reached out with inky hands.
"Be Still my child."
My discomfort, my resistance to comply,
a source of amusement to the infinite sky.

"You are a child of the divine, be still,
observe the seasons passing by.
Everything that lives, dies in time."

The wheel of life lifts and spins
and draws me in to timeless weaving.
Warp and tack, there and back.
Seasons turn too fast to track.
Yet each day is a new beginning
born from the centre.

A spark is lit, a flame at my feet,
spins a fire hurricane,
burns my flesh until nothing remains.

"Be Still my child" he says again.
"But how? " I cry.
"Can I be still when fire rages, and war blazes,
I can see the grief on people's faces
While a planet dies."

"This time is for being,
for living and breathing,
not seething in rage. So be still."

And there in the eye of the fire,
No space, no movement. Divine sent,
I find once more, my core, my strength.

The breath of life from earth,
through me and back to the sky.
Together, we sigh.

Like snowdrop spears break through the ice,
before their heads can bow in prayer.
It is there.

Stillness.
Nothing is like it was before.
Sword drawn I step into the dawn.

Gerroff My Leyline!

"Gerroff my leyline!" he shouted.
In a spectacular display of anger.

He scared the tourists,
Expectation of sacred space crumbled,
Dissolved as chalk in water.

Wild as a hedge monkey, he was.
Ready to chase off the war drums.

Yesterday, he hummed a sweet tune,
Harmony through cider rouged smiles,
Happy as a boar in springtime.

Today he is protector of dragon lines.

He hates the sacred space full
Of ceremony and nakedness.
Today he feels blessed, he is pissed,
Unbridled, prowling and wild
Stalking the leylines.

Can You Keep a Secret?

The keeper of the diary,
holds every providential date.
Each moment, peaceful sanctuary,
til she opens up the gate.

An empty ledger of measure,
means naked new moon phases,
full holy days of reverence,
a treasure full of fulfillments pages.

Crisp and clean, the days advance
unswayed, until the phone rings.
Then a diary, dog eared by demands,
fills up the weeks with things.

Tell no-one of the empty page.
She covers it with busy ness.
An illusion,
just a clever way
to keep some precious days
of nothingness.

The Road that Tam Lin Took

The poet only saw two roads,
One less travelled and one untook.
The third, to him was quite unknown.
The winding path that Tam Lin roamed,
Through elven Glade and faery nook.

Of all the roads that he might take,
And right before his path was set,
He stood and look and looked and stayed,
Yet missed the road in the forest glade
And chose to choose regret.

Frost never spied the Faerie Queene
Come dancing through the yellow wood.
Did she intend to go unseen?
Or did the poet fail to dream,
And doze as faery poets should?

Now when I go a wandering,
I know to seek the hidden path,
And when I find the Faery King,
I'll go and to the Greenwood sing,
I do not fear unseelie wrath.

For I did swim the blood red spring,
And tended well the white,
And I did dance in fairy rings,
Dined in the court of the Summer King,
And feasted through the night.
Yes, I followed Tam Lin's path,
With all my worth and all my will,
And I did find the milk White Hart,
I stayed and made a love that lasts,
And built a home beneath that hill.

I Don't Believe in Fairies

I don't believe in fairies,
I know that they exist.
Last night I followed Gwyn Ap Nudd
out hunting in the mist.

I don't believe in goddesses,
I know them all too well
and I go with Brigid's blessings;
know her touch, her taste, her smell.

I don't believe in Almighty God,
yet I see It every day,
Divinity in everything
when I follow nature's way.

I don't believe in anything
and that's because I know,
believing in the weather man,
won't increase the chance of snow.

The Way to the Realm of Fae

Forget about the usual geography.
This landscape is not your typical topography.
Up may be down, left may be right,
light may be found in the midst of the night.

Dawn may be dusk, fall may be spring,
winter or summer, and who is your King?

So how do I get there?
Cunning folk ask.
Start off by sitting down on your arse.
You don't need that baggage,
set it down by the door.
Sink into the weight of your feet on the floor.

Feel the wet in your mouth and delight in the moisture,
the heat in your belly, like lighting a torch.
Take a lungful of breath, and that is not all.

Know the sky is above you, the Earth is below.
Relax into the stillness and let yourself go.
Beyond time and imagining.
Beyond bones and skin.
Beyond every concept that was boxing you in.

Follow the beat of the wild heart drum.
Look for your Fetch when the journey's begun.

Awake the Lady of the Lake

Sword of the East, a breath of wind to trust.
By vernal yew that shades the flowing spring,
A sacred blade left in the lake to rust,
To mourn the passing of the wounded king.

Where willow bark by ivy's envy clings,
And coils around the bladder of the fish,
Where well is covered by bisected rings,
A King defied by Merlin's secret tryst,
When Lady hid the wizard in the mist.

Spear of the South, a fire in the head,
Aroused the bard to speak with skilful tongue,
A story told, the words have all been said,
The story of Prometheus is done.

And thus the golden Bardic Chair was won.
The poet danced with rhyme and words of glory;
No need to take the fire from the sun.
Just Awen, revelry in myth to culture story.

Cup of the West, the grail that claimed the host,
And brought a living legend to this land.
To hear the Mother cry for Holy Ghost,
Water holds a memory - shifts the sand.

And as nature falls to industry's demand,
There deep within the land swells red and white,
Waters rising up as earth commands,
In peace, protect the water from her plight.

Rock of the North, the stone of sovereignty.
The seat by which the Royal liars fail,
For silence roars a pensive prophecy,
When the Stone of Destiny declines to wail.

That rock no longer graces Tara's vale,
Nor in Scone, twixt shores of mighty flood,
Since in Westminster Abbey it's regaled
You cannot squeeze the stone out of the blood.

Lift up the sword, prepare the crowns and thrones,
For knights who fought and thought they lost their way,
Who crossed the perilous bridge to go alone,
Where myth still lives and legend plays.

For Kings and Wizards, timely, will return
Awakened by the Lady of the Lake.
By breath and heat, by feather, blood and bone.
I call to you. Awake, awake, awake!

Jack in the Green

Have you seen Jack in the Green?
I don't know where he's gone.
Thought I saw him in the summertime,
Dressed up as Barleycorn.

Then cut and sheathed he had to leave,
How sorrowful we mourned.
Til All Soul's Eve, he won reprieve
As Jack O'Lantern's light reborn.

I fear he's lost in old Jack Frost,
When hoary bites the morn.
But young Green Jack
comes bounding back,
To blow the Beltane horn.

Call Me

Call me Air,
Cool white clarity,
Let me wrap you in my breeze,
Breathe into me.

Call me Fire.
Colour me red,
Let desire run free,
Walk all over me.

Call me Water
Blue ripple of sea,
Rise and fall with the tides,
Dive into me.

Call me Earth,
Colour me green,
Rest your heaviness upon my lap,
Dig fingers in me.

Call me Up,
On the moonbeams,
To dance in the stars,
Fly with me.

Call me Down,
On bones of sweet memory,
To hear Ancestor stories.
Dig deeper with me.

Call me In,
Where all that's about me
Is seeded within,
Love me.

Printed in Great Britain
by Amazon

13971856R00062